STAY IN SCHOOL!
STAY OUT OF PRISON!

DAVID STUART SCHOFIELD,
PRISONER #334387

Resource Publications, Inc.
San Jose, California

Reprint Department
Resource Publications, Inc.
160 E. Virginia Street #290
San Jose, CA 95112-5876
1-408-286-8505 (voice)
1-408-287-8748 (fax)

Library of Congress Cataloging in Publication Data
Schofield, David Stuart.
    Stay in school! stay out of prison! / written and illustrated by David Stuart Schofield.
        p.   cm.
    Summary: Discusses the many unpleasant consequences of going to jail, including the negative aspects of life on Death Row and in other areas of prison.
    ISBN 0-89390-366-3 (pbk.)
    1. Juvenile corrections—United States. 2. Prisoners—United States—Social conditions. 3. Juvenile delinquency—United States—Prevention. 4. High school dropouts—United States—Prevention.
    [1. Prisons. 2. Prisoners.]   I. Title.
    HV9104.S326   1997
    364.36'0973—dc21   97-11268

Printed in the United States of America

01 00 99 98 97 | 5 4 3 2 1

Editorial director: Nick Wagner
Editor: Ken Guentert
Prepress manager: Elizabeth J. Asborno
Production assistants: Mike Sagara, David Dunlap, RuthAnn Stolzman

Contents

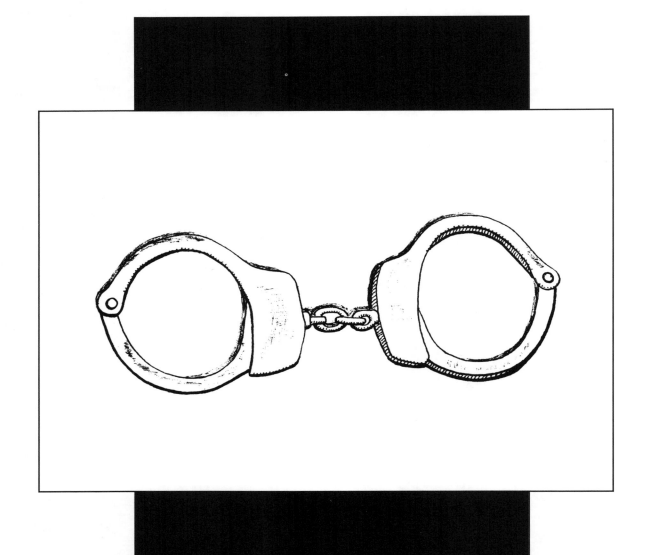

STAY IN SCHOOL!
STAY OUT OF PRISON!

Dropouts—Headed for Prison!

There are nearly fifty-six million school dropouts in America. Almost one million Americans are prisoners in America's jails and prisons. About sixty percent of the prisoners are illiterate.

Before deciding to drop out of school, students should think about the following facts.

Nearly ninety-thousand convicted teenagers are under control of federal and state courts in America by being in prison or on parole.

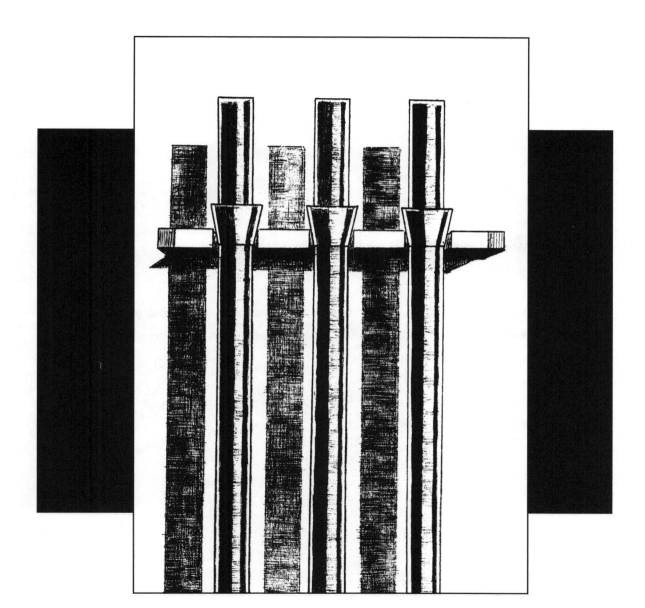

Most prisoners in jails and prisons are school dropouts—six out of every ten!

About six hundred thousand school dropouts—teenagers and adults—are numbered among the more than one million prisoners in America's jails and prisons.

School dropouts are more likely to be sent to prison, sooner or later, than school graduates.

Death Row!

"Death Row" describes the parts of prisons where prisoners with death sentences are kept. About five hundred teenagers in America have death sentences. Almost two thousand older prisoners are also on death row.

Thirteen states allow the execution of teenagers. Twenty-three other states allow the execution of adults only.

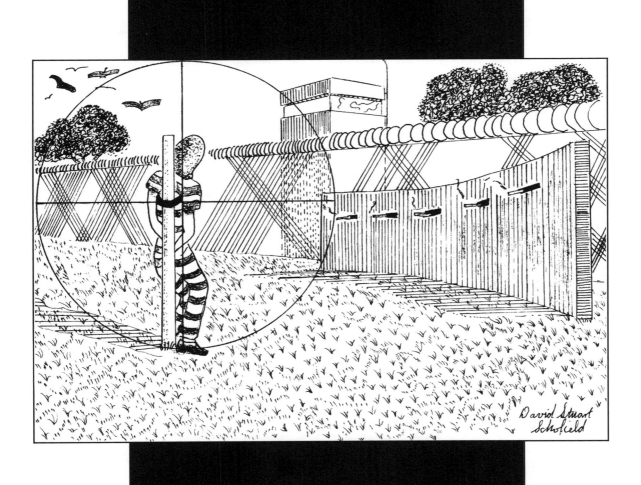

David Stuart
Schofield

Legal ways states can kill prisoners with death sentences are by electric chair, lethal injection, gas chamber, firing squad, and hanging.

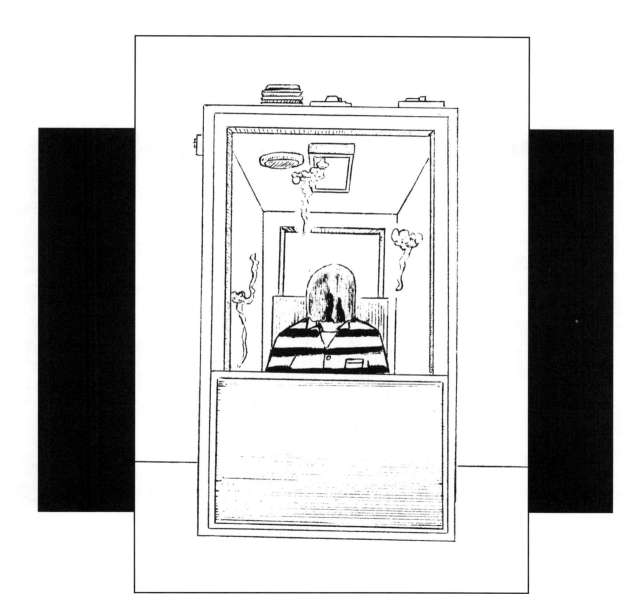

Other Ways to Die in Prison!

Prisons are dangerous places. Some prisoners are killed by other prisoners during fights and riots. Some of the ways prisoners can be—and have been—killed by other prisoners include stabbing, hanging, burning, starvation, and being beaten to death.

And prisons are hazardous to your health. It is easier to catch AIDS and T.B. in prison than it is in the outside world.

Suicide is the cause of death for some prisoners. In fact, prisoners are more likely to kill themselves than people who aren't in prison.

Still another way some prisoners die behind bars is death from natural causes. A prisoner with a life sentence will probably die in prison of old age if he is not paroled first or killed.

Prison is no place to die—or live.

Boot Camps and Other Lock-Ups!

Boot camps are a recent idea for locking up teenagers. Almost nine thousand inmates are held in the fifty-eight boot camps in America. Fourteen states have boot camps for young female inmates, too.

Boot camps are modeled after military training camps and confine young, non-violent offenders. The boot camp routine is a mixture of work, discipline, drills and training, loosely similar to prisons.

Some boot camp programs follow boot camp itself with confinement in halfway houses and home confinement. Violent lawbreakers and older offenders go straight to prison.

Still other forms for confining teenagers are called reformatories or reform schools, or youth homes or youth ranches. They are all forms of imprisonment.

Crime Doesn't Pay—It Costs!

By staying in school and learning to make a living legally, graduated former students are less likely to break the law to make ends meet. And students who graduate from school make more money during their lives than school dropouts do. Making fewer dollars is another cost of dropping out of school.

To defend himself in a courtroom, a prisoner must spend thousands of dollars on attorney's fees. Just buying snacks and writing materials from jail and prison commissary stores can cost more than a thousand dollars a year. Not all prisoners have relatives who can afford to send related prisoners that much money. Most prisoners become absolutely broke during confinement.

It's Smarter to Stay in School!

Dropping out of school, breaking the law, and getting sent to prison is not only expensive and dangerous; it is also not too smart. Only two percent of the American population ever goes to jails or prisons. Ninety-eight percent of Americans are smart enough to obey the law and stay free.

Only two percent of Americans weren't smart enough to know they'd be caught if they broke the law.

For the sake of their own futures, students must stay in school and graduate.

Prisoners Are Losers!

Anyone who thinks freedom is all a convict can lose by being sent to prison is wrong. Read on. What follows is a list of things a convict loses with just one conviction.

Prisoner's Losses:

1. Freedom;

2. A few years—or a lot of years—off the convict's life;

3. Safety;

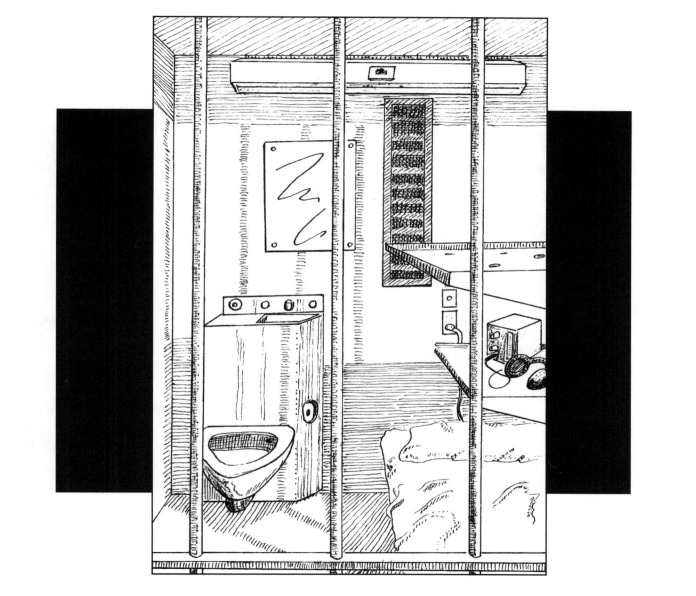

4. Hygiene;

5. Health;

6. Credibility;

7. Reputation;

8. Social acceptability, influence;

9. Employability and earning power;

10. Credit rating;

11. Income;

12. Right to vote;

13. Privacy;

14. Individuality;

15. Self-respect and self-esteem;

16. Pleasant and nutritional food;

17. Restful sleep;

18. Loss of money due to attorneys' fees and day-to-day prison costs such as the prison commissary;

19. Sanity (some prisoners lose their minds);

20. Long life span (normal life span might be shortened by prison-caused trauma or disease);

21. Life itself due to death sentence or long "life" sentence, death due to other natural causes, or suicide or murder;

22. Hope and optimism;

23. Freedom of choice and other non-prison opportunities;

24. Opportunity to associate with members
of the opposite sex;

25. Customary conveniences such as warm water
to shave with!

Prisons Cause a Smaller World!

Friends of some prisoners desert them. Some convicts' relatives might desert them, too. For convicts the entire world begins to shrink and leave them alone.

To make matters worse, first-time offenders are sometimes forced to join prison gangs. Expensive. Some prisoners are forced to let gangsters make decisions for them.

The new prisoner drafted by the gangs might soon find that his property is confiscated for the greater welfare of the gangs. Some prisoners are forced to work for the prison gangs and for the gangs' associates in the outside world.

Relatives and friends of some prisoners might also be endangered by prison gangs and the gangs' outside world connections.

A convict's relatives and friends might be robbed and their homes burglarized.

Female friends and female relatives of the newly convicted prisoner might be harmed.

A convict might discover that by breaking the law, he endangered everyone he knew.

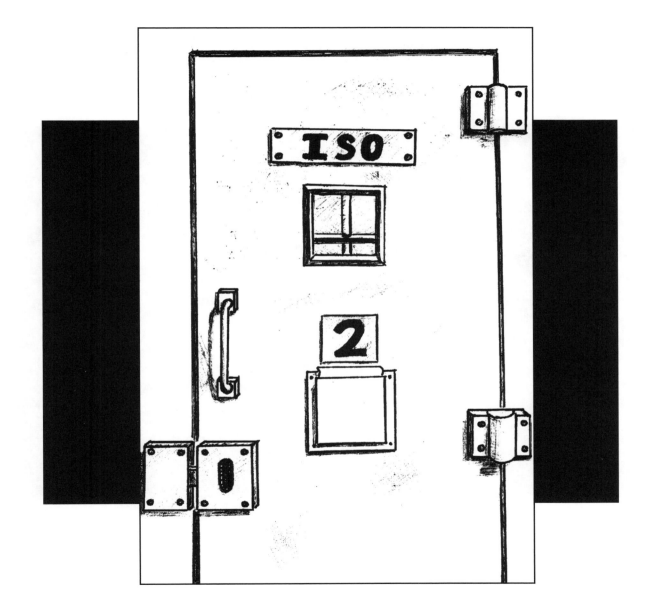

Lawbreakers give their own families black eyes. Convicts become the skeletons in their families' closets.

Prisoners become social lepers, and their families might share the public blame and embarrassment.

More about Life in Prison

Many prisoners speak their own language. Slang. They use this slang to confuse unwanted listeners in crowded prisons. The language is often ugly and violent.

Many convicts in prisons expect to die behind bars—at least they are aware of that possibility. Many of them are broke and broken and have become hapless slobs with no futures. So they've lost self-respect and respect for others.

Some prisoners get involved in the arts, thinking they can make money this way. Other prisoners ridicule such convicts as "the art force."

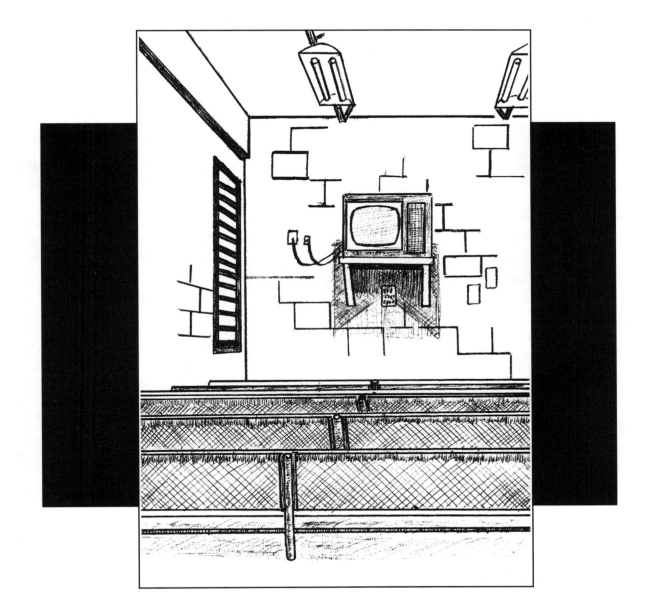

Sooner or later prisoners learn that medical care in prison is not only impersonal but also indifferent. There is no such thing as preventive medicine. Crisis management is the rule. Some states even charge a fee to prisoners whenever they need medical care.

Convicts are aware of their low-man-on-the-totem-pole status. They often become so estranged and alienated that they need psychiatric care. When prisoners lose their minds, psychiatrists often insist on giving the prisoners large doses of psychotropic medicine, which can cause physical tics or jerking and tremors.

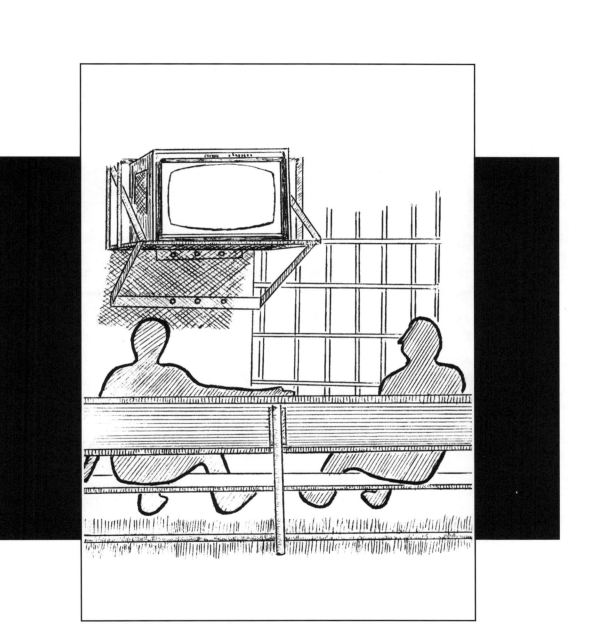

In prison, preoccupation with death is commonplace. There are often jokes about this. In prison slang, "Dade County" (a county in Florida) means dead, as in "the living and the Dade."

Murder and torture victims, inside and outside of prison, become the butt of jokes.

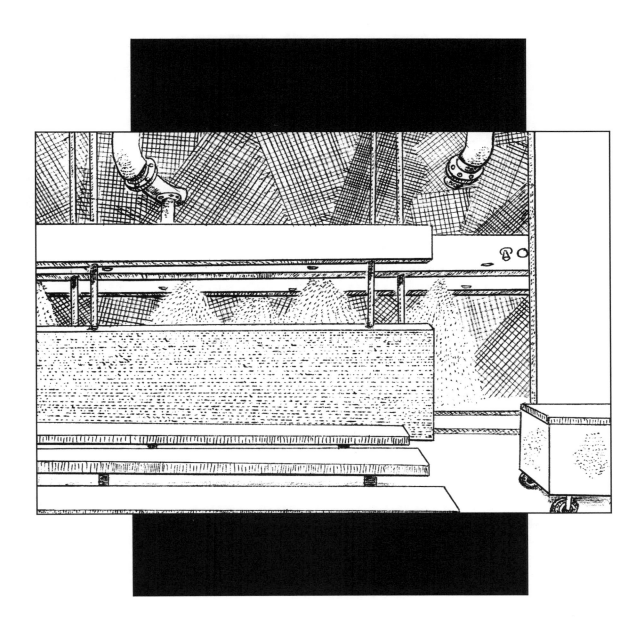

Only occasionally is there a hint that prisoners hold out the hope for a better life somewhere. One expression used is "got ach du himmels" from the German for "For heaven's sake!" This is used when a prisoner dies and, however unlikely, goes to heaven.

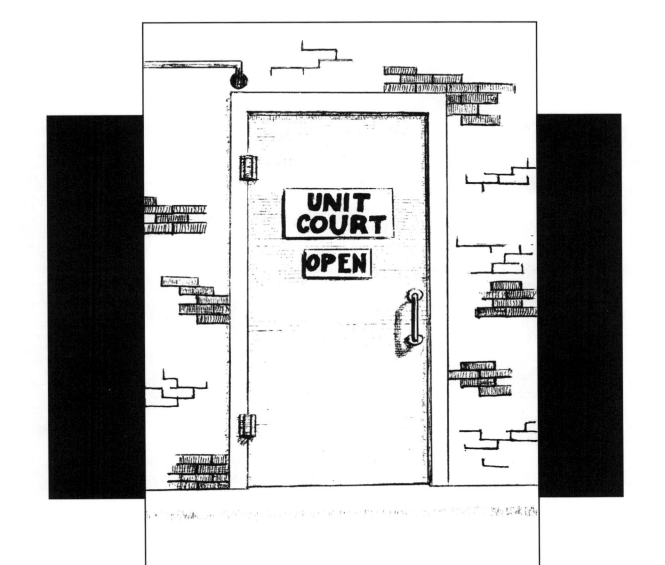

Prisoners like nicknames, even for someone who dies. There is one for someone who is burned to death and another for someone who bleeds to death, alone in a cell.

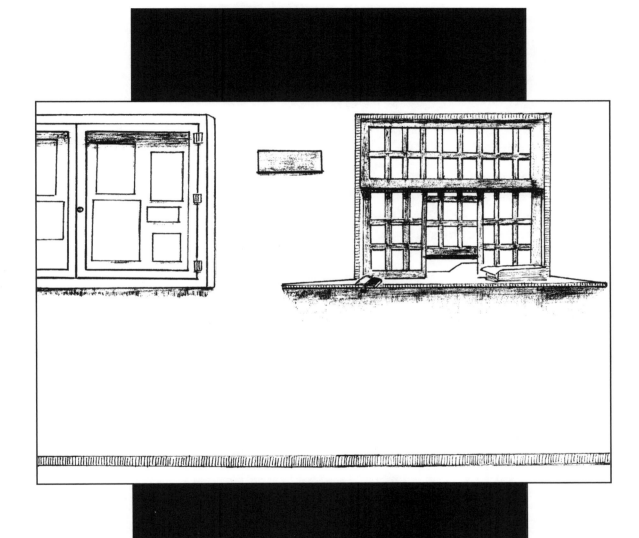

Noise is constant. Prison slang reflects this. A nickname for a torture victim is "howls."

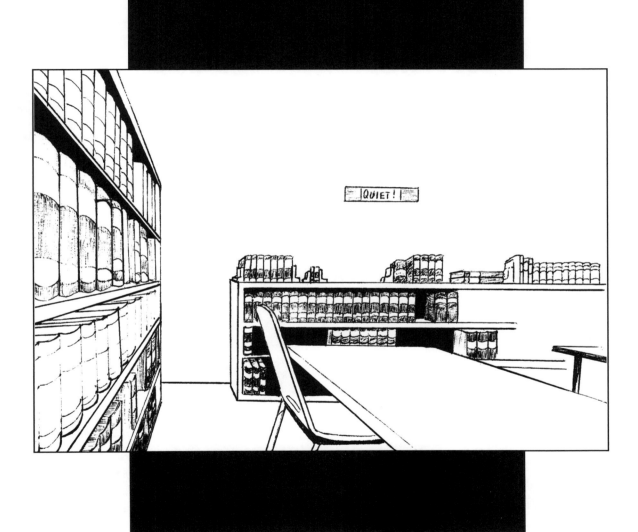

In prison, even simple pleasures are twisted. For example, references to food are likely to be slang for bodily waste.

Prison is a place where even die-hard enemies—men who literally want to kill each other—are crowded together. In prisons nightmares can easily come true.

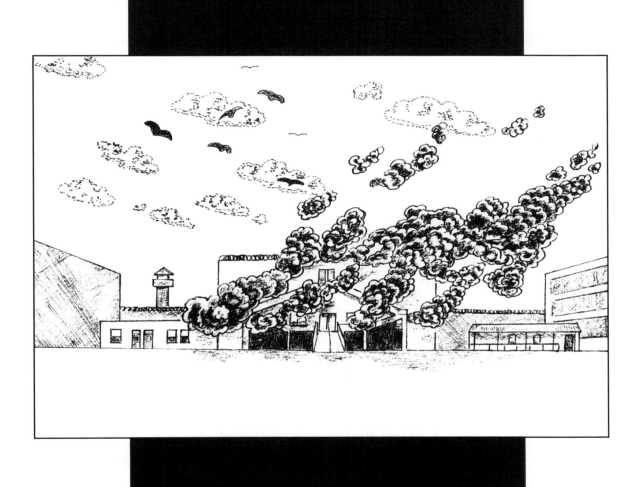

Often there is a "rack up"—an order for all prisoners to return to their bunks or "racks" and stay there. This can last a long time.

Gangs levy "sin taxes" on behavior they don't like. Of course, they have their own definitions of sin.

In prison there is little dignity beyond church services. Some prisoners could often be found searching ash cans for cigarette butts. That was stopped in a Texas prison when cigarette smoking was outlawed and the tobacco supply dried up (1995).

The higher density of swindlers behind bars makes it dangerous for any prisoner to deal with other prisoners. Officially such deals are prohibited by rules against "trafficking and trading." But some black markets are rumored to exist.

A Final Word

America's correctional institutions hold 1.5 million prisoners. Nearly one-tenth of them are juveniles. New prisons and boot camps are being built every year to lock up even more prisoners. There is always room for more. Don't join them!

References

Statistical Abstract of the United States Bureau of Prisons,
via General Services Administration

Encyclopedia Americana

FACING VIOLENCE
Discussion-Starting Skits for Teenagers

R. William Pike

Paper, 192 pages, 6" x 9", ISBN: 0-89390-344-2

Teens have many reasons for acting up. Trouble at home. Trouble with relationships. Trouble on the streets. You can get them to talk about their problems and explore solutions by using simple dramas. *Facing Violence*, part of the *Acting It Out* series provides you with 40 skits addressing violence in schools, violence in the home, violent language, violence and dating, violence and bias, violence in society, and solutions. Try them. They work!

FACING SUBSTANCE ABUSE
Discussion-Starting Skits for Teenagers

R. William Pike

Paper, 192 pages, 6" x 9", ISBN: 0-89390-374-4

Tobacco. Alcohol. Drugs. These substances threaten the lives of teenagers today. The danger comes not only from how they themselves use controlled substances but from the prevalence of abuse among their families and friends. Teenagers need to know how to respond. With these real-to-life skits, which can be performed without props or rehearsal, you can get young people to work out practical ways to respond to the substance abuse in their lives. Contains more than 40 skits which have been developed and tested. They work.

STREET SMARTS
Activities that Help Teenagers Take Care of Themselves

Dr. Michael Kirby

Paper, 80 pages, 8½" x 11", ISBN: 0-89390-331-0

Somehow teenagers must learn how to make it in the hazardous world of work and adulthood. They have to learn how to take care of themselves. This book examines the many roadblocks in their way and helps them explore how to overcome them. Case studies, role-plays, and activities involve them in the process and make the learning fun. A great resource for a variety of small group settings. Could be used as a course or as pick-and-choose activities. Includes permission to photocopy handouts.

Call Toll-Free 1-888-273-7782 for current prices.
See last page for ordering information.

Discussion Starters

ACTING IT OUT
74 Short Plays for Starting Discussions With Teenagers

Joan Sturkie and Marsh Cassady, Ph.D.

Paper, 358 pages, 6" x 9", ISBN: 0-89390-178-4

Getting teens to talk about their feelings and personal experiences can be frustrating. *Acting It Out* offers a new approach: Teens act out a short play, then discuss how the characters deal with the particular issue. Questions at the end of each drama help articulate issues and feelings. These dramas address challenging subjects: abortion, suicide, child abuse, gangs, anorexia, home life, drugs. Issues are presented in a straightforward manner and your teens are encouraged to talk about them in the same way.

ACTING IT OUT JUNIOR
Discussion Starters
for 10-13 Year Olds

Joan Sturkie and Marsh Cassady, Ph.D.

Paper, 160 pages, 6" x 9", ISBN: 0-89390-240-3

This book is similar to the popular *Acting It Out* collection except that these 48 skits address issues important to younger people: abuse, alcoholism in the family, dating, drug abuse, gang activity, homosexuality, cheating, shoplifting, and more.

PLAYS TO PLAY WITH IN CLASS

Sally-Anne Milgrim

Paper, 208 pages, 5½" x 8½", ISBN: 0-89390-060-5

This book is an example of transactional literature — it invites students to respond to the text out of their own values, morality, and experience. Contains eight original one-act scripts with accompanying language arts activities.

THE PEER HELPING TRAINING COURSE

Joan Sturkie and Maggie Phillips

126 looseleaf pages, 8½" x 11", ISBN: 0-89390-311-6

Teenagers often find it easier to talk about their problems and issues with other students. By helping teens identify and talk about their issues, peer helpers also learn something about themselves. And a peer helping program can help improve school attendance which helps with the overall grade point average.

A revised and expanded version of *The Peer Counseling Training Course*, this is a complete curriculum and teacher's guide for a high school course, which can also be used with some junior high school students. Four new chapters have been added to this edition.

The Peer Helping Training Course helps teens learn how to be there for each other. The practical training course is divided into two sections. Part one (units 1 - 9) introduces the skills students need to be good communicators. Part two (units 10 - 23) deals with specific problems such as peer pressure, drugs, death, AIDS. Appendices contain a sample letter to parents of peer helpers, glossary, community resources, and an excellent bibliography.

THE PEER HELPER'S POCKETBOOK

Joan Sturkie and Valerie Gibson

Paper, 104 pages, 4" x 7", ISBN: 0-89390-237-3

Everything needed for effective peer support is here: review of basic communication skills, counseling tips, synopsis of information on issues, and a section for important referral telephone numbers — for those times when more help is indicated.

The Peer Helper's Pocketbook is a quick and easy guide written for peer helpers/counselors on the junior and senior high school levels as well as college. This small book has proven helpful in both empowering and instructing students. It has come to symbolize responsible peer helping among students everywhere. Put a copy in the faculty room because it is a handy reference for faculty, counselors, and parents.

The Peer Counselor's Pocketbook, contains the same basic information as *The Peer Helper's Pocketbook*. It is the original edition, which was written by consultant Joan Sturkie and peer counselor Valerie Gibson for those involved in peer counseling programs. (ISBN 0-89390-162-8)

The two books listed above are both available at bulk discount prices. Give a copy to each of your peer helpers and help them better understand their role, the skills they need, and the referral information that is so important to what they do.

Call Toll-Free 1-888-273-7782 for current prices.
See last page for ordering information.

LEADERSHIP SKILLS FOR PEER GROUP FACILITATORS

Joan Sturkie & Charles Hanson, Ph.D.

Paper, 144 pages, 5½" x 8½", ISBN: 0-89390-232-2

Master the skills you need for successful group leadership with this handy guidebook, including the following: setting up groups, recognizing stages of growth within a group, communicating effectively, connecting group members, and empowering the group to accomplish its goals.

Character Education

CULTIVATING CHARACTER
Parent-Teacher Resources
for Grades 9, 10, 11, and 12

Richard K. Buchholz

Stapled, illustrated, photocopiable pages, 32 pages, 8½" x 11"
ISBN: 0-89390-407-4 (Grade 9)
ISBN: 0-89390-406-6 (Grade 10)
ISBN: 0-89390-405-8 (Grade 11)
ISBN: 0-89390-404-X (Grade 12)

How do you instill good character in young people? According to Richard Buchholz, you keep it simple. You get teachers and parents to work together. And you use lots of praise. With his *Cultivating Character* resource books, you use these principles to prepare young people to become good parents, workers, and citizens. Each book contains a "thought for the month" master, along with background information, that can be photocopied and posted on bulletin boards, given to students for hanging in lockers or keeping with their personal journals, and mailed to parents for posting on refrigerator doors. With constant repetition — Bucholtz recommends 20 times a day — the "thought for the month" can have a powerful effect on the behavior of a young person. Simple. Easy. And effective.

THE EMPOWERING SCHOOL:
Getting Everyone on Board to Help Teenagers
William L. Fibkins, Ph.D.

Paper, 160 pages, 5½" x 8½", ISBN: 0-89390-330-2

Everybody knows teenagers are in trouble. William L. Fibkins says it's time to stop looking for scapegoats and do something. The school can be the difference — if *everyone* gets on board. Fibkins calls this — the empowering school." He has seen his own school turn teenagers around and says yours can, too. He takes you through the seven steps required to set up an empowering school. Then he shows you how empowering-school principles have been used to set up support programs for teenagers addicted to tobacco, alcohol, and other drugs and for teenagers affected by eating disorders or family crises.

William L. Fibkins is a national trainer, consultant and keynote speaker. Founder of the Shoreham-Wading River Middle School and High School Student Advisory and Student Assistance Program, he received his master's degree and doctorate in educational counseling from Syracuse University. He has more than 30 years experience counseling in secondary and middle-school settings.

THE TEACHER-AS-HELPER TRAINING MANUAL
William Fibkins, Ph.D.

Looseleaf with tabs and binder, 250 pages, 8½" x 11", ISBN: 0-89390-411-2

As budgets tighten, counselors need all the help they can get in the fight to keep at-risk teens from going over the edge. This manual helps you enlist teachers as your allies and train them to help students effectively and safely. In the first part of the book, you'll learn how to prepare to sell teachers on the helping concept. In the second part of the book, you'll find all you need for a one-day in-service in which you explain the helping concept, listen to teacher concerns, admit the pitfalls, and stress the importance of professional training in helping skills. In the third part of the manual, you'll find a series of in-services that teach basic helping skills, how to help students safely, and how to apply helping skills to various problems. Author is available for — training the trainer" workshops.

Call Toll-Free 1-888-273-7782 for current prices.
See last page for ordering information.

Controlling Foul Language

WHAT TO DO WHEN YOUR STUDENTS TALK DIRTY

Timothy Jay, Ph.D.

Paper, 160 pages, 5½" x 8½", ISBN: 0-89390-363-9

Abusive language creates all kinds of legal, social, and interpersonal problems in schools. Finally you can do something about bad language on your campus. *What to Do When Your Students Talk Dirty* promotes teacher awareness of abusive language and shows them how to reduce the problem on campus. The book gives strategies specific to cursing, profanity, blasphemy, obscenity, sexual harassment, vulgar language, insults and ethnic slurs, scatological language, and slang. It stresses cognitive-behavior strategies and practical ways of reducing bad language. Use this book together with the companion book for parents to reduce bad language at school and at home.

"...well organized, clear, informative, and comprehensive. It provides valuable insights into student behavior and methods for dealing with unwanted language. Reading the book forces a teacher to look more closely at his or her own language and value system."

— Carol Cain, Middle School Teacher.

WHAT TO DO WHEN YOUR KIDS TALK DIRTY

Timothy Jay, Ph.D.

Paper, 160 pages, 5½" x 8½", ISBN: 0-89390-412-0, November 1997

Timothy Jay, author of *What to Do When Your Students Talk Dirty*, has followed up with this companion book for parents. Like the original, this book starts by defining the types of bad language — from vulgarity to obscenity to insults — and then sets out to help readers control bad language in their environment. In this case, in the home. Jay shows parents how to clarify which language values are important to them and then he shows them how to use proven behavior management techniques to improve the quality of their children's language. Useful for parents of children of any age, including teenagers. Use this book together with the companion book for teachers to reduce bad language at home and at school.

Timothy Jay, a professor in the psychology department of North Adams State, is widely quoted in the national media as an authority on cursing and bad language. His previous books are *Cursing in America* and *What to Do When Your Students Talk Dirty*.

Call Toll-Free 1-888-273-7782 for current prices.
See last page for ordering information.

SO, WHAT IS ASSERTIVENESS?
An Assertiveness Training Course

Chrissie Whitehead

Paper, 64 pages, 8½" x 11", ISBN: 0-89390-296-9

Aggressive vs. assertive. What's the difference? This book clarifies the difference between assertive and aggressive behavior, emphasizing that assertive behavior brings about acceptable results to all involved. You'll appreciate the easy-to-use lesson plans and photocopiable handouts which lead to identifying and changing patterns of aggressive behavior. And you'll like the author's ideas for setting up and promoting the course, too. The lessons can be taught as a separate course, worked into a self-esteem or life-skills course, or they can be used in less structured situations in youth or neighborhood groups, teacher in-service, adult education programs or business offices.

LOOKING IN, REACHING OUT
A Manual for Training Service Volunteers

Dorinne Thomas

Looseleaf with binder, 192 pages, 8½" x 11", ISBN: 0-89390-376-0

Service Learning is a wonderful process, but volunteers need to be trained to ensure that they — and those they are assigned to help — have good experiences. This manual is a complete, ready-to-go course for training service volunteers in school or community settings. Part one focuses on developing self-awareness and preparing them emotionally for service work. Part two focuses on development of such specific skills as listening, asking questions, responding, problemsolving, decision-making, and giving feedback. Part three focuses on building group identity and collaboration skills. All activities have been thoroughly tested over several years. Looseleaf format has everything you need to train service volunteers, including handout masters with permission to photocopy.

Dorine Thomas is an occupational specialist and peer-counseling chair at Buchholtz High School in Gainesville, FL. She has an advanced degree in counseling from the University of Florida.

FINDING THE WORK YOU LOVE
A Woman's Career Guide

Astrid Berg

Paper, 216 pages, 6" x 9", ISBN: 0-89390-269-1

If you or someone you know is exploring work options, use this manual to pinpoint your unique skills and workstyle so that you can pursue the occupational field best suited to you. This book is packed with information and exercises that will lead you to identify the work you love. Once you've focused your interests and used the author's tips for researching career and educational opportunities, then read the final chapter on decision-making. Homemakers, professionals, college students — all women in career transition — your search will be more complete (and the results more satisfying!) if you work through this guide first.

After re-entering the workforce and returning to school for her Master's degree in counseling, Astrid Berg decided to use her experience to help others make their own career and life transitions. She teaches college-level courses in career planning and counseling, and she practices private career counseling. Author and publisher of several career development resources, she currently lives with her husband and son in San Francisco, California.

BALANCING YOUR LIFE
Setting Personal Goals

Paul Stevens

Paper, 96 pages, 4¼" X 7", ISBN: 0-89390-375-2

The key to improving your life, according to noted "worklife" expert Paul Stevens, is planning. All you need is privacy, peace and quiet, a pad of paper, and lots of enthusiasm. *Balancing Your Life: Setting Personal Goals* provides that extra push. It will help you sort through the conflicting issues you deal with each day, the opportunities you want to explore, and the actions you need to take to bring balance to your life. In the end, you'll emerge with a set of clear personal goals that help you balance career with the rest of your life.

Call Toll-Free 1-888-273-7782 for current prices.
See last page for ordering information.

Grief Resources

HEALING OUR LOSSES
A Journal for Working Through Your Grief

Jack Miller, Ph.D.

Paper, 104 pages, 7" x 10", Illustrated, ISBN: 0-89390-255-1

In *Healing Our Losses*, the author shares experiences of loss in his own life and will guide you to record your memories, thoughts, and feelings about the loss in your life. Ample journaling space is provided. Working through this book will comfort anyone who has suffered the loss of a loved one and will help them to eventually heal their pain. Journaling may be done alone by an individual or in a group setting.

"...Jack Miller's work is immensely valuable... His concept of making a tribute to a loved one is wonderful..."

— Baroness Vera von der Heydt, author of *Prospects for the Soul: Soundings in Jungian Psychology and Religion*

"Jack Miller has enabled people to address areas of repressed, unresolved grief and conflict which have been gnawing within them for many years."

— Fr. Anthony Gatt, St. Vincent de Paul Presbytery, Southampton, England

DREAMS THAT HELP YOU MOURN

Lois Hendricks

Foreword by Wayne E. Oates, Professor of Psychiatry Emeritus, University of Louisville

Paper, 176 pages, 5½" x 8½", ISBN: 0-89390-395-7

You don't expect losing a loved one to be easy, but you're still not prepared for the dreams. The violent dreams. The macabre dreams. The erotic dreams. The guilt-inducing dreams. Even the joyful dreams can be deeply upsetting — especially if you're not expecting them. *Dreams that Help You Mourn* puts you in company with other mourners and their dreams. You'll learn that dreaming after losing a loved one is absolutely normal. In fact, it's the soul's way of mourning. You'll find out you're not alone — and you'll be able to take better advantage of the healing power of your dreams.

Lois Hendricks gives hundreds of examples of dreams — gleaned both from her own interviews and from literature. In so doing, she shows that every dream serves a purpose. This book will be a powerful comfort to the grieving — and a useful referral book for counselors and therapists.

Call Toll-Free 1-888-273-7782 for current prices.
See last page for ordering information.

RISING ABOVE
A Guide to Overcoming Obstacles and Finding Happiness

Jerry Wilde, Ph.D.

Paper, 144 pages, 5½" x 8½", ISBN: 0-89390-345-0

Everyone experiences some setbacks, losses, or health problems. Such events can be opportunities for growth. Pain can be a good friend asking you to change. This book by a psychologist who had to face his own life-threatening disease, lays out some tools that will help you face any dilemma with a minimum of suffering. Great referral book for counselors.

Jerry Wilde received his doctorate in educational psychology from Marquette University. Currently, he works as a school psychologist, a college instructor, and a psychotherapist in private practice. He is a proponent of Rational Emotive Behavior Therapy and has written several books. He lives with his wife and child in the Milwaukee area.

Stories for Children

HEARTWAVES
Daily Meditations for Children

Mary S. Burnett

Paper, 192 pages, 5½" x 8½", ISBN: 0-89390-396-5

Here's a resource that can support children ages 7-12, especially those who are in emotional pain. *Heartwaves* is a daily meditation book, written with simplicity and wit by a school counselor. The 366 stories are based on fact, many of them word for word from children, and are indexed alphabetically by subject. The simple, concrete examples introduce children to such healthy concepts as "setting boundaries" and "detaching" in relationships. Reflections following each story gently suggest a solution to the problem and affirm the child's experience. The author takes a gentle spiritual approach, nudging children toward trusting a higher power operating in their lives. Common themes appearing throughout the book include: respect your feelings, reach out to others, change what you can. A great tool for support groups. Useful for a broad range of children, from those living with fundamentally healthy families to those living in difficult circumstances.

"Mary Burnett has used the process of reflection in a powerful way by offering young people an opportunity to respond to specific examples and situations with which they can relate. Counselors, teachers, parents and other caregivers can use these stimulating meditations as a springboard to a variety of helpful conversations and activities with young people."

— John M. Lane, Ph.D., chairman of Behavioral Studies and Educational Technology department, University of South Alabama

HEROES, REBELS & SURVIVORS
Mostly True Tales about Growing Up

Larry Castagnola

Paper, 128 pages, 5½" x 8½", ISBN: 0-89390-365-5

For children who have outgrown Mother Goose, here is a book of 15 stories with positive moral content. Each story makes a moral point and is designed to help young people start to make the transition into adulthood. Includes stories such as "How the Weeping Willow Got Its Name" and "A Butterfly on a Bald Man's Head." The stories can be read by the children themselves or by a teacher. Discussion questions make it easy to use in small group settings. Designed for children ages 9-13 years old.

Call Toll-Free 1-888-273-7782 for current prices.
See last page for ordering information.

STORYTELLING STEP BY STEP

Marsh Cassady, Ph.D.

Paper, 156 pages, 5½" x 8½", ISBN: 0-89390-183-0

If you tell stories for any reason — or want to — this is the book for you. Marsh Cassady, a gifted storyteller and drama instructor, takes you through all the steps: selecting the right story for you, selecting the right story for your audience, adapting your story for different occasions, analyzing it so that you can present it well, preparing your audience, and presenting your story. Along the way, he includes 23 examples of stories that can be told.

CREATING STORIES FOR STORYTELLING

Marsh Cassady, Ph.D.

Paper, 144 pages, 5½" x 8½", ISBN 0-89390-205-5

This book picks up where the author's popular *Storytelling Step by Step* left off. Includes ideas for creating your own original stories, adapting stories to different audiences, plotting a story, creating tension, and writing dialogue that will keep your listeners on the edge of their chairs.

Order from your local bookseller, or contact:

 Resource Publications, Inc.
160 E. Viriginia Street #290
San Jose, CA 95112-5876
1-408-286-8505
1-408-287-8748(FAX)
Order Toll-Free:
1-888-273-7782
www.rpinet.com
orders@rpinet.com